Original title:
Snooze and Cruise to Dreamland

Copyright © 2024 Creative Arts Management OÜ
All rights reserved.

Author: Juliette Kensington
ISBN HARDBACK: 978-9916-90-394-0
ISBN PAPERBACK: 978-9916-90-395-7

Swirls of Midnight Magic

In the depth of night so deep,
Stars awake from their silent sleep.
Whispers dance on moonlit air,
Enchanting dreams beyond compare.

Colors blend in cosmic sway,
Mysteries of night at play.
Veils of shadow softly glide,
As secrets of the dark abide.

Lullaby of the Cosmos

Cradled in the velvet sky,
Galaxies spin and softly sigh.
Planets hum their ancient tune,
A lullaby to stars and moon.

Nebulae wrap in tender light,
Flowing gently through the night.
Each twinkle sings a soothing rhyme,
In the arms of space and time.

Navigating Dreamy Waters

Sailing through the realms of dreams,
Where nothing is as it seems.
Waves of thought, both calm and wild,
Carry whispers soft and mild.

Moonbeams shimmer on the sea,
Guiding hearts to sets them free.
In the stillness, time stands still,
Navigating with gentle will.

The Gentle Voyage Home

As the sun dips low and red,
The path ahead is gently spread.
Each breath whispers tales of old,
Of journeys sweet, yet bold.

Harbor calls with open arms,
Embracing warmth, the heart charms.
Softly we drift through twilight's hue,
Finding peace in skies so blue.

Resting in the Crook of Night

In shadows deep, the stars do gleam,
A hush descends, a gentle dream.
Night embraces, soft and tight,
I find my peace in the crook of night.

Whispers float on cool, dark air,
Caressing thoughts, a tender care.
Each heartbeat fades, a soothing flight,
Lost in the calm of moonlit sights.

Moonbeam Pathways to Hypnos Land

Through silver trails, the night unfolds,
A pathway bright where dreams are sold.
Each step I take, a soft command,
Leading me to Hypnos Land.

In twilight's glow, I drift away,
To realms where night gives birth to day.
With every breath, the shadows stand,
Welcoming me to Hypnos Land.

Echoes of the Sleeping Breeze

In whispered tones, the breezes sigh,
A lullaby beneath the sky.
They wrap around like gentle hands,
Echoes soft where silence stands.

Each rustling leaf, a secret shared,
A melody of love declared.
In every breath, the world demands,
To listen close to sleeping bands.

Journeys Beyond the Waking World

In dreams I soar, away I fly,
Past clouds of thought, through velvet shy.
Worlds unfurl with each blink's swirl,
Journeys vast beyond the pearl.

Through starlit gates, my spirit twirls,
In cosmic dance, where magic whirls.
Each heart's desire at twilight's cue,
Journeys await, adventures new.

The Sleepy Sailor's Guide

Anchor your thoughts, let worries drift,
The moon whispers secrets, a gentle gift.
Stars twinkle softly, a lullaby's hum,
Sailing through night, where dreams come from.

The tides hush the world, all is at peace,
Close your eyes tightly, let troubles cease.
The compass of slumber points true to the heart,
A voyage of rest, where we all play a part.

In the Arms of the Dreaming Sea

Beneath silver waves, where quiet resides,
The ocean's embrace is where calm abides.
Whispers of lullabies echo through night,
In the arms of the sea, all feels so right.

The currants bring dreams, soft as the air,
Floating on clouds, with not a care.
Nautical visions swirl like the tides,
In the arms of the sea, every heart glides.

Sail Away to the Land of Nod

Open your sails, let the sea call your name,
The Land of Nod waits, never quite the same.
With stars as our guide, we'll drift through the night,
Sail away, dear sailor, to dreams taking flight.

The horizon whispers, where wonders abound,
In slumber's embrace, new joys can be found.
Close your eyes gently, let the journey unfold,
As waves rock your boat, find the magic, be bold.

Woven Dreams and Starry Nights

In the fabric of dreams, stardust is sewn,
Every wish, a thread, so lovingly grown.
Underneath twilight, magic ignites,
Woven dreams soar through starry nights.

A tapestry sways, with colors so bright,
Each moment, a spark, igniting the night.
With a heart full of hope, let your spirit take flight,
Embrace all the wonders of the beauty in sight.

Beyond the Sleeping Horizon

A whisper of dawn on the edge of night,
Where dreams linger softly, a delicate flight.
The stars fade slowly, a gentle retreat,
While shadows stretch wide on the cool, damp street.

In the hush of the morning, the world stands still,
Embracing the magic that dawns with a thrill.
With colors unfolding in hues soft and bright,
The horizon awakens, banishing fright.

Birds take to the sky in a jubilant rise,
Their songs weaving tales, a sweet, soft surprise.
Each moment a treasure, too precious to keep,
As life stirs around us, rousing from sleep.

Beyond the horizon where dreams softly play,
Each heartbeat a promise, each breath a ballet.
We dance with the light in this tender embrace,
Beyond the sleeping horizon, we find our place.

A Midnight Expedition

In shadows we wander, beneath the pale moon,
The world holds its breath, like a still, ancient tune.
With whispers of secrets tucked deep in the night,
We chase after echoes, in search of the light.

The stars are our compass, twinkling and bright,
Guiding our footsteps through the mystery's might.
With hearts full of wonder, we journey afar,
On this midnight expedition, under a star.

The cool breeze a blanket, wrapping us tight,
As laughter erupts, sharing joy and delight.
We delve into stories of old and of new,
Each step a discovery, each moment true.

When dawn gently beckons, as night slips away,
We hold onto memories that never decay.
For in the night's magic, we found a way,
A midnight expedition, in hearts here to stay.

Slumber's Silken Sails

In the cradle of night where the soft shadows dwell,
Slumber drapes visions, a shimmering spell.
With silken sails drifting on waves made of dreams,
We float through the quiet, where starlight redeems.

The moon casts her glow like a guardian's embrace,
Guiding lost wanderers to their destined place.
Each breath is a whisper, a lullaby's call,
As slumber's soft vessels carry us all.

In the depths of the night, our worries take flight,
The tapestry woven of moments so light.
With hearts intertwined in a blanket of peace,
Through slumber's silken sails, all troubles will cease.

When morning arrives, with its golden intent,
We wake from our journey, our spirits content.
With dreams as our treasure, we rise and we sail,
On the winds of tomorrow, with slumber's soft trails.

Drifting on Moonlit Waves

Beneath the stars, the waters gleam,
A silver path, a sailor's dream.
Whispers of wind gently sway,
Guiding hearts as they drift away.

Lapping shores in soft embrace,
Carried forth by time and space.
Horizon kissed by night's cascade,
Secrets in the moonlight played.

Whispered Lullabies of the Night

Softly sung by evening's breeze,
Melodies that put hearts at ease.
Crickets play their serenade,
In the dark, fears start to fade.

Gentle glow of the distant star,
Promises of peace from afar.
Wrapped in dreams, the world feels right,
Lost in whispered lullabies of the night.

Floating on Cloud Nine

In the realm where dreams take flight,
Bubbles of joy dance in the light.
Colors swirl in a boundless sky,
Hope flutters by, oh so high.

Joyous laughter fills the air,
Weightless hearts without a care.
Each moment feels like pure delight,
Floating softly, all is bright.

The Journey through Midnight's Portal

A shimmering gate of silver hue,
Through the night, the wanderers flew.
Secrets of time whisper near,
Echoes of dreams that draw us near.

Stars align in a cosmic dance,
Guiding souls with a gentle chance.
Into the depths where shadows play,
The journey begins, come what may.

Whispering Tides

The moonlight dances on the sea,
Whispers of waves call out to me.
Gentle swells and foamy sighs,
Underneath the vast, dark skies.

Footprints fade on sandy shores,
As ocean hymns play, evermore.
Shells hold secrets, tales of old,
In their curves, the mysteries unfold.

Sails are filled with dreams untold,
As the night hangs its cloak of gold.
Stars above, they gleam and glide,
In this dance, I drift with the tide.

Serenity in the Stars

In the stillness of the night,
Stars twinkle with soft, sweet light.
Whispers of cosmic tales untold,
In their glow, I feel consoled.

The vast expanse, a tranquil sea,
Where dreams float, wild and free.
Each glimmer holds a wish, a prayer,
In the silence, I find my care.

Galaxies swirl in silver hues,
Guiding wanderers with their clues.
In the dark, I lose my fears,
Beneath the stars, I shed my tears.

Floating with the Fireflies

Among the trees, they softly glow,
Tiny lanterns in evening's flow.
With each flicker, stories weave,
Glimmers that the night believes.

Dancing softly on the breeze,
Their light brings joy and gentle ease.
Underneath the twilight hue,
Magic stirs, as dreams come true.

I reach out to join their flight,
In the calm embrace of night.
Together we drift, a bright display,
As moments melt and fade away.

The Gentle Current of Night

A soft breeze whispers through the trees,
Carrying secrets, a playful tease.
The shadows dance, the night's embrace,
In twilight's calm, I find my place.

Ripples glide on the silver pond,
Reflecting dreams of dusk's response.
In the stillness, I hear the sighs,
Of distant stars in velvet skies.

Time flows gently, like a stream,
In the quiet, I dare to dream.
With each heartbeat, shadows play,
In the quiet night's gentle sway.

Daylight's Goodbye

The sun bows low, a final glow,
Casting shadows long and slow.
Whispers of night begin to stir,
As the daylight starts to blur.

Stars emerge, a twinkling dance,
In the dark, we take our chance.
Holding memories, soft and bright,
As we bid adieu to light.

A Soothing Farewell

Softly spoken, tender tone,
In the twilight, we're not alone.
Kindred spirits share a smile,
A moment's peace, if just a while.

Warm embraces, gentle sighs,
As we part beneath the skies.
Echoes linger in the breeze,
A soothing farewell that brings us ease.

The Opal Sea of Dreams

Waves of opal, glint and gleam,
Carry us to realms unseen.
In every ripple, stories flow,
Of whispered hopes, and dreams aglow.

Floating softly, time stands still,
In the depth, our hearts fulfill.
A canvas painted with desire,
The opal sea, our souls aspire.

Margaritas at Midnight

Under stars, the night unfolds,
With laughter rich, and stories bold.
Margaritas chilled, a perfect blend,
In this moment, we transcend.

Sips of joy, with salt's embrace,
Every taste, a warm embrace.
As midnight whispers sweet goodbyes,
We chase the dreams beneath the skies.

Embracing the Dreamworld

In twilight's gleam, the dreams arise,
With whispers soft beneath the skies.
They beckon hearts to drift away,
To worlds where night becomes the day.

In shadows deep, the secrets dwell,
A tapestry of joyful spell.
Embrace the visions, let them soar,
Unlock the magic, seek for more.

Where stars collide with hopes anew,
Each wish we make finds form and view.
In dream's embrace, we learn to fly,
Leaving behind our worries high.

With every sigh that blends with night,
We paint our fears with colors bright.
In dreamworld's arms, we find our place,
A sacred realm of soft embrace.

Voyage to the Land of Whimsy

A ship of clouds sails through the air,
To lands where laughter fills the square.
Each wave a giggle, each breeze a cheer,
In whimsy's land, there's naught to fear.

With candy hills and rivers wide,
We dance on rainbows, side by side.
The sun giggles, the moon winks bright,
As we chase dreams in pure delight.

The trees wear hats, the flowers sing,
Each step a joy, each glance a fling.
In this domain where all is free,
We find our hearts in jubilee.

As day begins to fade away,
We treasure moments, sweet and gay.
To whimsy's land, we'll always roam,
A place forever, calling home.

The Night's Dreamy Soiree

When night descends, the stars align,
A soiree waits, so sweet, divine.
With moonlit glow, we spin and twirl,
As dreams unfold, our hearts unfurl.

The music sways like whispers soft,
In rhythm, we drift, our spirits loft.
The night, a canvas, painted deep,
Where laughter lingers and secrets seep.

With every glance, a story told,
In dreamy hues, our minds behold.
The world asleep, yet here we play,
Forever lost, yet found, we stay.

So let the night be our friend true,
In every heartbeat, every view.
At this soiree, we'll dance till dawn,
Our dreams entwined, forever drawn.

Port of a Thousand Dreams

At twilight's gate, we find a shore,
Where dreamers gather, seeking more.
Each wave that breaks, a whispered sigh,
In the port where all our hopes can fly.

With lanterns bright, in colors bold,
Stories of wishes, yet untold.
Each ship that sails brings hopes anew,
Crossing the sea of skies so blue.

The stars like guides, the moon our king,
In this haven, our hearts take wing.
With every breeze, we cast our fears,
For in this port, we shed our tears.

As dawn approaches, dreams take flight,
From shore to sky, we chase the light.
In this port of dreams, we are free,
A thousand visions, eternity.

Soothing Shadows of the Night

Whispers weave through moonlit trees,
The gentle breeze brings sweet reprise.
Stars wink softly, secrets shared,
In the night, our dreams are spared.

Silvery beams on silken streams,
Crickets sing of quiet dreams.
Wrapped in night's dark velvet cloak,
Time drifts by, a tender joke.

Clouds drift by in shadows deep,
Nature's lullabies invite sleep.
In the calm, we find our peace,
In darkness, every worry cease.

So as we rest under vast skies,
Let soothing shadows close our eyes.
The night, a friend, forever near,
In its embrace, we hold no fear.

Ethereal Wanderlust

Footprints cover distant lands,
With open hearts and outstretched hands.
Every step a new embrace,
In every corner, find a trace.

Mountains tall and oceans wide,
In every moment, worlds collide.
The horizon calls with a song,
Leading us where we belong.

Wanderlust in every vein,
Through the sunshine, through the rain.
Each adventure a sacred rite,
Chasing dreams that feel so right.

Stars above, the stories told,
In whispers of the brave and bold.
Through every journey, ever blessed,
In wanderlust, we find our quest.

Rhythms of Rest

Gentle waves kiss sandy shores,
A peaceful pulse forever endures.
Nature hums a soft refrain,
In restful realms, we break the chain.

The ticking clock begins to fade,
In quiet moments, we are made.
Beneath the deep and watchful skies,
We find solace, where silence lies.

Eyes closed tight, we take a breath,
In every stillness, we feel left.
The world retreats, and time unwinds,
In rhythms of rest, true peace we find.

So take this pause, let worries cease,
In fleeting seconds, discover peace.
Rest your heart, let shadows dance,
Embrace the beauty of sweet chance.

The Softest Voyage

Sailing on a sea of clouds,
In twilight's hush, the heart enshrouds.
Gentle waves of muted light,
Guide the soul through starry night.

With whispered breezes, dreams take flight,
In the calm, we dare to write.
Every wave holds tales untold,
In every promise, futures bold.

On horizons painted soft and warm,
In every heartbeat, find the charm.
Let currents pull us through the deep,
In the softest voyage, we shall leap.

So close your eyes and drift away,
Let the night transform the day.
In this journey, ever free,
Find the voyage that's meant to be.

A Sailor's Reverie in Starlight

Upon the waves, a whisper flows,
Under the moon, where silence grows.
Stars above in a velvet sky,
Guide my heart as the night drifts by.

The rhythm of the ocean's sigh,
Carries dreams where the seagulls cry.
Beneath the veil of twilight's grace,
I find my home in this sacred place.

With every ripple, a tale unfolds,
Of brave adventures and hopes untold.
The sea, a canvas of shimmering light,
Paints my soul in the hush of night.

A sailor's heart, bold and free,
Finding solace in the endless sea.
In starlit reverie, I am one,
With the ocean's song, till night is done.

Dreamweaver's Tranquil Voyage

Softly the tides wash over the shore,
Whispers of dreams in a muted roar.
Clouds drift by with a gentle sigh,
A tranquil voyage where hearts can fly.

The hues of dusk wrap the world tight,
Mingling shadows with the fading light.
Each wave a story, calm and sweet,
In the heart's harbor, where souls meet.

With every breeze, I sail afar,
Chasing reflections of the evening star.
In the embrace of a tranquil night,
I dance with dreams in their soft flight.

The sea, a mirror of moonlit grace,
Carries me to a serene place.
On this voyage, my spirit roams,
Finding solace in ocean's homes.

Twilight's Gentle Embrace

Softly the twilight descends on the bay,
Cradling the world in shades of gray.
The sun bids farewell with a golden gleam,
As night in its beauty begins to dream.

Stars twinkle gently in the dark sky,
Like whispered secrets that never die.
They twirl and dance in the midnight air,
Inviting the heart to pause and stare.

The cool breeze sways the quiet trees,
Carrying the scent of memories.
In twilight's embrace, shadows play,
Telling stories in a hushed array.

With each moment, the night unfurls,
Wrapping the world in its silken pearls.
In the stillness, a sense of grace,
Finds a home in twilight's embrace.

Waves of Sleep

Gentle waves lap against the shore,
Whispering songs of dreams galore.
As darkness weaves its soothing spell,
In tranquil waters where echoes dwell.

The stars blink softly, like a lullaby,
Guiding the weary with a gentle sigh.
Cradled in arms of the ocean's sweep,
I drift away on waves of sleep.

The moon reflects on the quiet tide,
In stillness, I let my worries slide.
With every ripple, I find release,
Embracing the night, a moment of peace.

In this embrace of cool, calm seas,
I surrender to the night's sweet breeze.
Waves of sleep wash over me,
Carrying whispers of what could be.

Shores of Serenity

On the golden sand, I wander free,
Footprints in rhythm with the endless sea.
Shells whisper tales of the ebb and flow,
Echoing secrets that only they know.

A gentle breeze stirs the ocean air,
Sowing calm within the heart's care.
With waves that cradle the day's retreat,
I find my peace in the twilight's beat.

The sun dips low, painting skies so bright,
Bathing the shore in a soft warm light.
Each moment lingers in soft embrace,
On the shores of serenity, I find my place.

As stars emerge and the night descends,
The ocean hums as the daylight ends.
In this haven, my spirit shall roam,
Finding solace in the sea's warm home.

The Voyage of Forgotten Sighs

Upon the waves, where shadows play,
Whispers drift in a lonely sway.
Forgotten dreams, like ghosts they roam,
Adrift in search of a distant home.

Beneath the stars, old tales ignite,
Tales of love and silent night.
Each breath a memory, soft and wide,
Sailing forth on the ocean's tide.

The compass spins, the heart will pull,
Guiding souls with a lantern's lull.
In the distance, a beacon glows,
A refuge found where the river flows.

So cast your fears to the salty sea,
Embrace the journey, set your spirit free.
For every sigh that's lost to time,
Is a treasure hidden in the depths of rhyme.

Lanterns of Light in the Dark

In shadows deep, where footsteps rest,
Lanterns flicker, a gentle guest.
They guide the weary on their way,
Through tangled paths where night holds sway.

Each glow a promise, a hope reborn,
A soft embrace at the break of dawn.
Illuminating tales of old,
Of hearts entwined and secrets told.

Through the veil, where silence sings,
These guiding lights on fragile wings.
They dance upon the winds of fate,
Reminding us, it's never too late.

So lift your eyes to the sky so bright,
Let lanterns lead you through the night.
For every fear that clouds your sight,
Can fade away in the gentle light.

A Celestial Drift towards Slumber

In twilight's arms, where dreams take flight,
Stars waltz across the velvet night.
A celestial drift in quiet grace,
Carried softly to a slumbering place.

Each heartbeat slows, a tender sigh,
As moonbeams weave through the midnight sky.
Whispers of dusk call sweetly near,
Cradling the soul, dissolving fear.

Through galaxies where wishes bloom,
Kisses of night dissolve the gloom.
Floating softly on stardust streams,
Awake to live within your dreams.

So close your eyes, let the silence steer,
To realms of wonder, away from here.
For every drift that hushes the storm,
Is a journey into a world reborn.

Serene Horizons of Drowsy Delight

At the break of dawn, the earth exhales,
Serene horizons on gentle trails.
In hues of gold, the day unfolds,
With whispers sweet as the new sun holds.

Each soft breeze carries a lover's tune,
Entwined with petals that greet the moon.
In this embrace, time seems to fade,
As peace descends in a calming cascade.

Drowsy delight in a sunlit gleam,
Nature weaves softly, a waking dream.
Where laughter lingers in summer's air,
And hearts unite, shedding every care.

So linger here beneath the sky,
Where gentle moments never die.
In these serene horizons bright,
Find joy anew in the morning light.

The Lavender Voyage

Sailing on waves of lavender hue,
The sky whispers secrets, soft and true.
Gentle breezes carry thoughts to explore,
While dreams unfurl on the ocean floor.

Stars twinkle brightly, guiding the way,
In the quiet of night, where shadows play.
The scent of blossoms fills the night air,
A serene journey, free from despair.

With each passing moment, horizons wide,
The heart finds freedom, the soul's purest ride.
In the embrace of twilight's gentle grace,
We sail through the lavender, a heavenly place.

Navigation of Tranquility

In still waters, a vessel glides,
As peace envelops, the spirit abides.
With every ripple, calm thoughts arise,
Reflecting the stars in tranquil skies.

The compass points to serene dreams,
Where laughter and joy flow in gentle streams.
Time slows down in this sacred space,
Navigation led by a soothing embrace.

The horizon blushes in hues of gold,
Stories of peace in the silence told.
Drifting through moments, a heart set free,
In the navigation of tranquility.

The Celestial Snooze

Nestled beneath the moon's soft light,
Dreamers drift into the heart of night.
Stars are pillows, the sky their bed,
In a cosmic embrace, restless thoughts shed.

Galaxies twirl in a peaceful dance,
Cosmic lullabies put minds in a trance.
Wrapped in stardust, the world fades away,
In the celestial snooze, we long to stay.

Whispers of the cosmos soothe the soul,
While the universe spins, losing control.
Time stands still, in this heavenly phase,
As dreams take flight in a starry maze.

A Cloudy Caress

Softly drifting on a cloud so rare,
Whispers of comfort linger in the air.
Gentle shadows gently embrace the sun,
In a world of gray, we merge into one.

Raindrops dance like notes on the ground,
Nature's symphony, a harmonious sound.
Through the mist, dreams can intertwine,
A cloudy caress, a moment divine.

Between the veils of silence and grace,
A tender connection leaves a trace.
In fleeting moments, we find our way,
Embraced by the clouds, come what may.

The Ocean of Restful Fantasies

Beneath the waves so softly play,
Dreams drift like boats on a gentle bay.
Whispers of peace carry me far,
To realms of solace, they serve as a star.

In twilight's embrace, the tides unwind,
Lapping at shores where hope is kind.
Calm waters greet the wandering mind,
In the ocean's heart, our dreams are twined.

Each ripple tells tales of what could be,
A tapestry woven in harmony.
With every splash, a story unfolds,
In the deep blue, our comfort holds.

As night cascades with silver gleam,
Lullabies dance in a tranquil dream.
A world awaits beyond the foam,
In the ocean's arms, we find our home.

Navigating the Serene Abyss

With a compass forged in quiet grace,
I sail the depths, a soothing space.
Bubbles rise in a calming flight,
Guiding me through the endless night.

Stars reflect on the water's face,
Each wave a whisper, a gentle trace.
Floating softly in the cool embrace,
Where silence blankets time and place.

Currents weave songs of peace to hear,
A symphony played for the willing ear.
In the abyss, fears start to dissolve,
Through the murky depths, we gently revolve.

Finding solace in the vast unknown,
In the depths of dreams, I am not alone.
With each stroke of the oars in time,
I navigate through this blissful rhyme.

Slumber's Soft Serenade

As twilight falls, the world turns dim,
I hear the hush, a gentle hymn.
In shadows deep where spirits glide,
Slumber's sweet serenade resides.

Moonlight bathes the slumbering land,
Caressing softly with delicate hand.
Each note a sigh, a tender kiss,
A lullaby sung in peaceful bliss.

Wrapped in dreams where wishes soar,
I drift away to a distant shore.
Gentle breezes whisper low,
Guiding the heart where calm waters flow.

In the arms of night, I find my way,
Toward realms of rest where the heart can play.
The stars keep watch, a glittering guide,
As I float on waves of soft, sweet tide.

In the Realm of Silent Tides

Upon the shore where whispers dwell,
I find a peace, a sacred spell.
The tides are silent, their secrets deep,
In the realm of night, I softly creep.

Gentle rhythms pulse through the air,
A soothing presence, serene and rare.
With each ebb, my worries fade,
In starlit silence, my heart is laid.

Moonlit waters dance with grace,
Every ripple a tender trace.
In the hush of night, my spirit glides,
Embraced by the calm of silent tides.

Echoes of dreams softly entwine,
In the stillness, the world feels fine.
Finding solace in nature's embrace,
In the realm of tides, I find my place.

Midnight's Royal Caravan

Under the moon's soft glow, they ride,
Whispers of dreams, on the night's tide.
Stars adorn the velvet sky,
As shadows dance and spirits fly.

A caravan of hopes and fears,
Echoes of laughter, distant cheers.
Glimmers of fate in their hands,
Wanderers lost in foreign lands.

Through deserts vast and mountains steep,
They seek the secrets that they keep.
Each step a story, ancient, bold,
In every heart, a tale unfolds.

With dawn approaching, secrets fade,
But in their souls, the dreams parade.
The night's embrace, a fleeting trance,
In midnight's caravan, they chance.

Gentle Waves of Dusk

Whispers of the sea at twilight's edge,
Softly lapping at the sandy ledge.
Colors bleed as the sun sinks low,
Embracing the night in a warm glow.

Waves carry tales from distant shores,
Of lovers lost and ancient wars.
The breeze hums softly as it flows,
Weaving through shadows, where magic grows.

Stars blink awake in the darkening sky,
Painting the world as day says goodbye.
Each wave a promise, a lullaby sweet,
Inviting the heart to find its beat.

As dusk settles on the ocean's face,
Every moment, a gentle embrace.
In the hush of the night, dreams awake,
Guided by waves that softly break.

The Horizon of Imagination

On the edge where sky meets sea,
Lies the realm of what could be.
Brushstrokes of colors yet untamed,\nIn the mind's eye, a world unframed.

Mountains rise and valleys fall,
In the whispers of creativity's call.
Every thought a vibrant hue,
Painting pictures, both old and new.

Ideas take flight, soaring high,
Chasing clouds in a boundless sky.
The horizon beckons, vast and bright,
Where dreams become the stars at night.

With every glance, new visions spark,
Illuminating the endless dark.
In the heart of dreams, we find our way,
Creating worlds where we'd love to stay.

Petals on a Pillow

Softly falling like a gentle sigh,
Petals drift beneath the sky.
Whispers carried on a breeze,
In the quiet, hearts find ease.

Each blossom holds a tale of old,
Of love and warmth, of dreams untold.
On the pillow, they softly lay,
Guarding secrets at the end of day.

Colors fade into the night,
As shadows dance in pale moonlight.
With every petal, hope is sewn,
In this sanctuary, we're never alone.

Hearts entwined with nature's grace,
In this sacred, peaceful space.
Petals whisper as we rest,
Embracing dreams, we are truly blessed.

A Relaxed Expedition

Beneath the open sky so blue,
The gentle breeze whispers through.
Waves of laughter fill the air,
Nature's beauty everywhere.

With each step upon the trail,
Stories echo, soft and frail.
Mountains rise with grace and might,
Guiding us into the light.

The river sings a soothing song,
Inviting us to travel along.
Underneath the shades of green,
A tranquil world, serene, unseen.

As the sun begins to set,
Parting gifts we won't forget.
Gathered moments, pure delight,
In our hearts, a spark so bright.

The Twilight Passage

As day surrenders to the night,
Colors fade, a soft twilight.
Stars awaken, shy and small,
Whispers of the evening call.

Shadows dance upon the ground,
With secrets waiting to be found.
The moon sheds silver on the way,
Guiding dreams where night will play.

Crickets sing a serenade,
In this hour, fears invade.
Yet hope glimmers, faint yet clear,
In the stillness, peace draws near.

Through the passage, softly glide,
In this moment, worlds collide.
Wrapped in magic, deep and grand,
Together, we will take our stand.

Dream Weaver's Haven

In a realm where wishes weave,
Every heart has tales to leave.
Clouds of laughter, threads of grace,
In this haven, time we trace.

Through the door of dreams we stroll,
Finding pieces of the soul.
Stars adorn the velvet skies,
In their light, true magic lies.

Floating on a gentle breeze,
In this place, we feel at ease.
Stories crafted, soft and bright,
Here, we hold our dreams at night.

With every dream, a spark ignites,
Shining through the endless nights.
Whispers of hope gently flow,
In the haven, love will grow.

Soft Hands of the Night

Night descends with tender grace,
Wrapping earth in a warm embrace.
Stars emerge, a calming sight,
Guided by the soft hands of night.

The moon spills silver on the lake,
Creating ripples, dreams awake.
Crickets chirp, a lullaby,
As shadows dance and softly sigh.

Wrapped in quiet, worlds align,
In the stillness, hearts entwine.
Embers glow in the firelight,
Filling us with warmth so bright.

In this magic, we unite,
Underneath the cloak of night.
Together, we'll embrace the dark,
Finding solace in the spark.

Ebbing into Nightfall

Shadows stretch across the ground,
As day fades softly into night.
Whispers of the breeze abound,
Embracing stars in gentle light.

The sky transforms with shades of gray,
While crickets sing their evening song.
With each moment, dreams hold sway,
As dark descends, we all belong.

A tranquil hush embraces all,
The world slows down, breathes in deep.
In this stillness, hearts enthrall,
Finding peace in twilight sleep.

So let the currents take their flight,
In fading hues of dusk's embrace.
We drift beneath the cloak of night,
As dreams unfold in boundless space.

Basking in Moonlight

Softly glowing, silver beams,
Dance upon the tranquil sea.
Each wave a whisper, lost in dreams,
Embracing all in harmony.

The world transforms beneath the glow,
All worries fade, the heart feels light.
In moonlit whispers, spirits flow,
United in the magic night.

Stars twinkle brightly in the dark,
As lovers stroll through fragrant air.
In every gaze, a lasting spark,
Together lost without a care.

To bask in moonlight, pure and bright,
Is to find solace in the now.
In nature's arms, we feel the height,
Of love's sweet promise, here and how.

Nighttime's Cozy Harbor

In the harbor, softly glows,
A refuge from the day's delight.
Through every window, warmth bestows,
A sense of peace throughout the night.

With gentle waves that kiss the shore,
Time weaves a tapestry of dreams.
In cozy corners, hearts explore,
The magic found in quiet themes.

Laughter dances in the air,
As friends gather by the fire's light.
In every story, love lays bare,
Found in the warmth of shared insight.

Nighttime wraps us in its grace,
A haven where our troubles cease.
In nighttime's arms, we find our place,
A cozy harbor filled with peace.

Dreamer's Respite

Close your eyes, the world will fade,
As twilight whispers softly low.
In gentle arms, your dreams are laid,
A sanctuary where you grow.

Clouds of silver drift above,
Carried on the winds of night.
Here unfolds the tale of love,
And stars ignite with pure delight.

As you wander through your mind,
A universe of endless grace.
Seek the treasures you can find,
In dreamer's respite, find your place.

So let the night embrace your soul,
As magic weaves its tender thread.
In dreams, you find your heart's true goal,
A path where all your fears are shed.

Floating into the Ether

In twilight's grasp, we drift and sway,
A gentle breeze, a soft ballet.
Stars emerge, a cosmic dance,
In silence, we embrace the chance.

Through velvet skies, our spirits glide,
Away from all, we turn the tide.
The moon it smiles, a beacon bright,
Guiding us through the endless night.

Whispers of dreams in softest hums,
As stardust falls, our journey comes.
With every breath, we blur the line,
Between the world and realms divine.

Together we float, no ground beneath,
In this vast space, love is the sheath.
With hearts alight, we chase the glow,
Floating into the ether's flow.

Nighttime Serenade

In the stillness, shadows play,
Crickets chirp, the night's ballet.
The silver moon casts soft delight,
While stars above twinkle bright.

A whispering wind, a sweet embrace,
Lulls the heart to a peaceful place.
Notes of night in harmony blend,
As twilight dances, time will bend.

Each moment holds a fleeting sigh,
As echoes of love drift and fly.
In this serenade, dreams take flight,
Carried softly through the night.

Underneath the vast expanse,
We lose ourselves in the night's romance.
Together we'll weave through moonlit tides,
In this melody, our love abides.

A Journey Beyond the Stars

With courage bold, we take our flight,
To realms unknown, beyond the light.
Galaxies call, a siren's song,
In unison, we both belong.

Through cosmic winds, our dreams will soar,
Past ancient worlds, forevermore.
Nebulae swirl in colors bright,
Guiding us through the endless night.

Time fades away, we lose all fear,
As starlit paths draw ever near.
In the depths, where secrets hide,
We find our truth, our hearts collide.

So take my hand, let's cross the veil,
In this vast sea, we'll write our tale.
With every star, our journey starts,
A voyage deep within our hearts.

Chasing Starlit Waves

Upon the shore, the night unfolds,
Echoing dreams as the tide beholds.
Beneath the stars, we run and play,
Chasing starlit waves till break of day.

Moonlight dances on the crest,
With every wave, we feel so blessed.
The ocean sings, a haunting tune,
As hearts unite beneath the moon.

With laughter bright, we fill the air,
In this sweet moment, free from care.
The salty breeze wraps 'round us tight,
As starlit waves embrace the night.

Together we'll weave through silver foam,
In this shared dream, we'll find our home.
With every tide, our spirits rise,
Chasing starlit waves under the skies.

Slumber's Gentle Embrace

In twilight's hush, the world slows down,
Stars begin to twinkle in the crown.
Whispers of night in soft caress,
Carrying dreams, a sweet recess.

Crickets sing their lullabies near,
While shadows dance without a fear.
Wrapped in comfort, we drift away,
To fields of silver where echoes play.

Gentle winds blow through the leaves,
Each breath a treasure the heart receives.
Rest now dear soul, the night is long,
In slumber's arms, we find our song.

A realm of peace, where worries cease,
Within this bliss, we find our peace.
Let go of burdens, hold tight to love,
In dreams we soar, on wings above.

Distant Shores of Twilight

Beneath the arch of fading light,
The waves caress the shore so bright.
Where sky meets sea in hues so grand,
We find our hearts, a timeless land.

Whispers of breezes tell a tale,
Of distant shores where dreams prevail.
Golden sands and skies of blue,
Invite our hopes to break on through.

Footprints linger where lovers tread,
As twilight's glow paints the riverbed.
With every wave that kisses land,
Our spirits dance, hand in hand.

The stars awaken, one by one,
Marking the journey that's just begun.
In twilight's grace, we find our way,
To distant shores where forever stays.

Wading through Dreamscapes

In twilight's glow, we softly wade,
Through dreamscapes woven, unafraid.
Each ripple whispers secrets bright,
Glimmers of hope in gentle light.

With every step, the world dissolves,
Lost in visions that time resolves.
Colors swirl in the evening air,
As worries fade, beyond compare.

The moonlight paints a silver trail,
Guiding our hearts as stars unveil.
With laughter shared and silence deep,
We chase the visions our souls keep.

Awake yet lost, in realms we find,
The magic dwells within our mind.
In dreamscapes vast, we rise and fall,
Forever bound, we conquer all.

The Restful Odyssey

A journey started, night unfolds,
Through valleys deep and tales untold.
With every breath, a chapter turns,
In restful odyssey, our spirit yearns.

Across the lands where shadows play,
We seek the dawn that lights our way.
With stardust dreams, we glide and roam,
In every heart, we find our home.

The path may twist, the road may bend,
But love's the lantern, our steadfast friend.
With gentle whispers guiding light,
Through darkest hours we find our sight.

As weary souls find peace tonight,
The stars above shine ever bright.
In every step, we choose to see,
The restful odyssey sets us free.

Sailing Through the Soft Haze

The morning mist wraps all around,
A gentle breeze whispers, soft and sound.
Sails unfurl, catching dreams anew,
On waters calm, we drift where skies are blue.

The waves embrace, a tender song,
Our souls take flight, where we belong.
Guided by stars that softly gleam,
We sail on whispers, lost in a dream.

Each moment glows with a golden light,
The world behind fades out of sight.
In soft haze, we find our way,
Through the dawn of a brand-new day.

Let the journey weave its magic fine,
As hopes and wishes intertwine.
Forever bound by the ocean's grace,
We find our place in this endless space.

A Night's Canvas of Rest and Wonder

Under the stars, the darkness sighs,
Filled with secrets of ancient skies.
A canvas bright with dreams untold,
Awaits the brave, the young, the old.

The moonlight dances on gentle waves,
Whispering stories of lost, brave knaves.
Each twinkling star a wish set free,
Painting the night with mystery.

Wrapped in tranquility, we lay down,
The weight of the world no longer a crown.
As slumber beckons, soft and deep,
We drift away, surrendering sleep.

In the hush of the night, our spirits soar,
Exploring the realms of evermore.
With every heartbeat, we fade into night,
In a canvas of rest, we find our light.

Drifting into Slumber's Haven

The day melts down in shades of gray,
Where shadows whisper the light away.
In the cradle of night, so soft and deep,
We find a haven to quietly sleep.

Moonbeams weave through the silken air,
Spreading magic with tender care.
In dreams, we wander, hearts unbound,
Finding solace where love is found.

Gentle sighs of the world asleep,
In this moment, our wishes keep.
Drifting slowly, calm and free,
Into the night's serenity.

With every breath, we softly glide,
To a place where calm resides.
In slumber's arms, we shall remain,
Till morning's light calls us again.

The Sweet Harbor of Ephemeral Dreams

In the twilight's glow, we find our way,
To a harbor where wild hopes sway.
Crafted by whispers, soft and warm,
This sweet retreat keeps us from harm.

The waves carry tales of time gone by,
As night unfolds, we gently sigh.
Ephemeral dreams that softly blend,
In this safe space where worries mend.

With hands held tight, we drift along,
In a world where we both belong.
Here, the laughter dances in the air,
Memories woven with love and care.

As stars shimmer in the midnight sea,
In this sweet harbor, we are free.
With every heartbeat, the night stands still,
In dreams embraced, we find our will.

Fluttering into Slumber

The stars begin to fade away,
As dreams come softly, here to stay.
With whispers light and shadows deep,
I find a calm, embrace of sleep.

The moon hangs low, a silver glow,
While crickets sing their evening show.
A gentle sigh, the world so still,
Embraced by night, my heart does thrill.

In cozy corners, shadows play,
As lullabies drift, softly sway.
I close my eyes, let go of fears,
And drift away as night draws near.

With every flutter, peaceful, sweet,
I journey where my dreams will meet.
In slumber deep, I lose all time,
In twilight's arms, I softly climb.

Voyage through the Night

Set the sails for night's grand quest,
With stars as guides, we'll find our rest.
Drifting on waves of silken air,
Adventure calls, it's time to dare.

Each twinkling star, a beacon bright,
Leading us forth into the night.
With whispers soft of dreams untold,
We'll brave the dark, be brave, be bold.

The moonlight glimmers on the sea,
A world of wonders waits for me.
As shadows dance and waves reply,
Into the depths of night we'll fly.

With each new breath, the journey flows,
Through hidden paths where starlight glows.
In wand'ring dreams, we'll find our way,
Together bound, we'll seize the day.

Celestial Lullabies

Hear the night sing sweet and low,
With melodies of stars aglow.
Each note a wish, a heart's delight,
As lullabies float through the night.

Dreamers drift on silver streams,
Wrapped in the warmth of gentle dreams.
In cosmic arms, they sway and sigh,
'Neath velvet skies where wishes fly.

Softly now, the universe hums,
A soothing balm as starlight comes.
Each twinkling spark, a lullaby,
A serenade that draws us high.

Close your eyes and feel the grace,
Of cosmic love in this vast space.
With every breath, let go of cares,
As sleep descends, joy's song declares.

Pillow Fort Adventures

In a fort of pillows, safe and sound,
Imagination knows no bound.
With covers draped like fortress walls,
We journey through enchanted halls.

A castle grand, a pirate ship,
Where magic stirs, we dream and sip.
With flashlights bright, we roam the night,
Our laughter echoes, pure delight.

Beneath the stars of blanket skies,
We dance with dragons, soar, and rise.
Each whispered word, a spell we cast,
In this snug haven, shadows pass.

So stay a while, in dreams abound,
In our sweet fort, adventure's found.
With friends beside, we'll face the dawn,
In pillow dreams, our magic's drawn.

Echoes of a Silent Breeze

In twilight's hush, whispers flow,
Carried soft, where shadows grow.
Faintly glides the evening sigh,
Touched by dreams that wander by.

Among the trees, secrets weave,
A melody that few perceive.
Gentle notes of night unfold,
Echoes wrapped in threads of gold.

Each rustle tells a tale old,
Nature's voice in breezes bold.
Silent stories softly tease,
Carried forth on twilight's breeze.

When stars emerge, the world stands still,
Every heart with wonder filled.
In silence, magic takes its flight,
Echoes linger into night.

Wandering through Clouds

Drifting high, a dreamer's grace,
Painting skies, a soft embrace.
Cotton trails where wishes soar,
Endless realms we can't ignore.

Floating past the sun's warm glow,
Chasing shadows, feeling slow.
Every puff a thought takes shape,
In this realm, our hearts escape.

A tapestry of white and blue,
Where every breath feels fresh and new.
Wandering through cloud's soft veil,
On whispered winds, we set our sail.

In this journey, we find peace,
A world where worries fade and cease.
Above the earth, we softly drift,
In clouds, our spirits gently lift.

The Moon's Gentle Pull

Silver light on waters gleams,
Guiding lovers' whispered dreams.
In the night, her glow so bright,
Draws us close with tender light.

Each phase tells a tale of old,
Secrets kept, and mysteries told.
Gentle tides feel her embrace,
In her pull, we find our place.

Softly she climbs the velvet sea,
A calming force that sets us free.
Night unfolds with her sweet thrill,
The stars align, time stands still.

Underneath her watchful gaze,
Hearts entwine in moonlit haze.
With each blink, she steals our breath,
In her light, we dance with death.

Beneath the Velvet Sky

The cosmos stretches wide and deep,
In its arms, the dreams we keep.
Stars like diamonds, shimmering bright,
Guiding souls through endless night.

Beneath the sky, the world stands still,
Hearts unite with hope and thrill.
Constellations weave our fate,
Underneath the stars, we wait.

A canvas dark, a story writ,
With every glance, as time is split.
Dreamers gather, hand in hand,
Within this vast and endless land.

Whispers swirl in midnight air,
Promises floated everywhere.
Beneath the velvet sky we gaze,
In starlit wonder, we are swayed.

A Calm Odyssey of the Mind

In the stillness of the night,
Thoughts like stars begin to shine.
Drifting softly, lost in dreams,
A journey flows, serene and fine.

Waves of wisdom, gently rise,
Echoes of the heart's soft sighs.
Maps unwritten, paths unfold,
Through quiet realms where truth abides.

Mind like water, deep and clear,
Reflects the world without a fear.
Each ripple tells a tale of old,
In whispers simmering, drawing near.

So sail within this tranquil sea,
Embrace the calm, let thoughts run free.
For every odyssey we find,
Begins within the depths of me.

Secrets Whispered by Evening's Tide

Beneath the hush of twilight glow,
Secrets linger, soft and low.
The ocean sighs, it breathes anew,
With stories wrapped in salty flow.

Each wave that kisses golden sand,
Carries whispers from the grand.
Promises hidden in the night,
By gentle hands, those tales are planned.

The moonlight dances on the sea,
A symphony of mystery.
With every tide, the heartbeats thrum,
In harmony, so wild and free.

As stars align, their secrets shared,
In twilight's arms, we're unprepared.
For all the dreams the ocean holds,
Are stitched in waves, so beautifully dared.

Whispers of the New Moon

In silence thick, the new moon waits,
A canvas dark, where hope creates.
Soft murmurs float on gentle air,
In shadows deep, the heart elates.

Gathered dreams within the night,
Glow with an ethereal light.
A chance to breathe, a moment pure,
As stars recede from fleeting sight.

Moonbeams sketch a path unknown,
Guiding souls to where they've grown.
With each embrace, the tender call,
To find the seeds of love we've sown.

Hold tight the whispers, soft and sweet,
In every breath, our lives complete.
For in the dark, the light will bloom,
The magic of the new moon's beat.

Driftwood Dreams

Along the shore where memories lay,
Driftwood sings of yesterday.
Each piece a story, worn but bold,
In whispers soft, they sway and play.

Tides that echoed laughter's song,
In sunlight's warmth, they once belonged.
Now scattered skies tell tales of hope,
Where hearts once danced, and dreams were strong.

Nature's art, both rough and fine,
Crafting beauty, like aged wine.
Every curve and weathered line,
Tells of journeys intertwine.

So gather 'round, let memories stream,
In every piece, a fragment gleams.
For driftwood holds the essence true,
Of all our whispered driftwood dreams.

Moonbeam Marmalade

In the jar of twilight glow,
Dreams are spread like morning rays.
Whispers of a night aglow,
Captured in sweet orange haze.

Stars shimmer with a playful tease,
As moonlight dances on the ground.
A taste of night, a gentle breeze,
Where savory dreams can be found.

Beneath the hush of slumber's song,
Marmalade kisses softly chime.
In this realm, we all belong,
Awash in blissful, quiet time.

Nights are bathed in golden glow,
Savoring the joys we hold.
With each bite, let our spirits flow,
In moonlit tales, forever told.

A Sojourn in Snooze

Close your eyes, the world can wait,
On a cloud, we drift away.
Dreams will weave a cozy fate,
In this peaceful, silent play.

Mountains rise and rivers flow,
In soft whispers, slumbers call.
Time suspends, and fears be slow,
Here in dreams, we have it all.

Gentle breezes kiss our thoughts,
Floating softly through the night.
In this realm, true joy is sought,
Sojourn here till morning light.

Every sigh, a soothing rhyme,
Dancing lightly, shadows weave.
In this quiet space of time,
Close your eyes, and just believe.

Celestial Driftwood

Under starlit skies we roam,
Drifting on the cosmic sea.
Celestial wood finds its home,
In the heart where dreams run free.

Each piece tells a story old,
Waves of time they softly keep.
In the silence, secrets unfold,
Whispers echo as we sleep.

Galaxies twinkle in our eyes,
Guiding us to shores unknown.
On this wood, the past still flies,
Echoing the love we've grown.

From the depths of night we rise,
Floating gently in the breeze.
Every breath, a sweet surprise,
Time suspended, hearts at ease.

The Undersea Nap

Beneath the waves, in deep repose,
Creatures dance in liquid light.
Where coral reefs in silence doze,
And dreams take flight beneath the night.

Anemones sway in harmony,
While soft whispers brush our skin.
In this realm of mystery,
Where the ocean's lullabies begin.

Echoes of the tide's embrace,
Flowing gently, calm and deep.
In this magic-vibrant space,
Undersea, we drift and sleep.

Time is lost in blue delight,
As we float on currents free.
In the depths, we find our sight,
Dreaming in our reverie.

Moonlit Reveries

In twilight's hush, the shadows dance,
A silver glow, a fleeting glance.
Whispers from the trees above,
Cradling dreams as stars do shove.

The night unfolds its velvet shroud,
Where secrets hide among the crowd.
Each twinkle speaks of tales untold,
In moonlit reveries, bright and bold.

Silver path on waters wide,
Guiding hearts where wishes hide.
The gentle breeze carries yore,
A symphony, forevermore.

As dawn approaches, dreams may fade,
Yet memories of night cascade.
In every heart, a light remains,
From moonlit paths and soft refrains.

The Sleepy Sailor's Tale

Upon the sea, the sailor drifts,
With tired eyes and misty lifts.
The waves, they hum a lullaby,
As stars above begin to sigh.

Every horizon tells a story,
Of distant lands and fading glory.
His ship, a cradle on the deep,
Where dreams and waves together leap.

With each soft splash, the night unfolds,
A tapestry of silver and gold.
He sails through realms of hazy night,
Guided by the moon's soft light.

In dreams, he finds his compass true,
With every star, a path anew.
The sailor sleeps, but hopes to find,
The shores where waking hearts unwind.

Navigating the Land of Nod

Through twilight's veil, we gently glide,
In the land of Nod, where dreams collide.
Each step a whisper, soft and low,
Guided by the starlight's glow.

Fantastical creatures greet the night,
In colors bold, with sheer delight.
They weave a world of whimsy rare,
In slumber's grasp, without a care.

Clouds like pillows, soft and wide,
Carrying thoughts on the ebbing tide.
With every sigh, a thought takes flight,
In the vast expanse of deepening night.

Awake we'll be, yet dreams abide,
Whispers of joy that we cannot hide.
In the land of Nod, we lose our way,
Only to find it come break of day.

Enchanted Nocturne

In the hush of night, enchantments wake,
With every breath the shadows shake.
A melody drifts through the air,
Softly calling, tender and rare.

Underneath the canopy wide,
Whispers of magic the stars confide.
Moonbeams stitch the seams of dreams,
Where nothing's ever as it seems.

Each rustling leaf, a gentle sigh,
In nocturnal realms, we learn to fly.
The nightingale sings a haunting tune,
Beneath the watchful, silver moon.

As dawn approaches, the spell will break,
Yet echoes linger, softly awake.
In the heart, the night will stay,
An enchanted nocturne, come what may.

Milton Keynes UK
Ingram Content Group UK Ltd.
UKHW021928011224
451790UK00005B/67